ROHAN CANDAPPA

The Little Book of
CHRISTMAS
STRESS

EBURY PRESS

First published by Ebury Press in Great Britain in 2003

1 3 5 7 9 10 8 6 4 2

Ebury Press
Random House · 20 Vauxhall Bridge Road · London SW1V 2SA

Random House Australia Pty Limited
20 Alfred Street · Milsons Point · Sydney · New South Wales 2061 · Australia

Random House New Zealand Limited
18 Poland Road · Glenfield · Auckland 10 · New Zealand

Random House (Pty) Limited
Endulini · 5A Jubilee Road · Parktown 2193 · South Africa

The Random House Group Limited Reg. No. 954009

www.randomhouse.co.uk

Papers used by Ebury Press are natural, recyclable products
made from wood grown in sustainable forests.

A CIP catalogue record for this book is available from the British Library.

ISBN 0 09 189456 5

Text design by Lovelock & Co.
Cover design by Two Associates

Printed and bound in Denmark by Norhaven Paperback A/S

Dedication

This is my tenth book in five years. A suitable point to thank the people who helped, encouraged or generally believed in me as a writer. Below I name the guilty parties.

Chris Liffen, who spotted a 'laconic sense of humour' in my last school report. Mike Coughlan, who gave me my first paid employment in adland. Polly McDonald, who never seemed to doubt that I had something to offer. Jack Rosenthal and Bruce Robinson for having the grace and generosity to encourage the efforts of those less talented than themselves. John Howard Davis for showing me the funniest way to fall. Susie Brookes Smith for getting me in to see her agent when I was getting nowhere. Simon Trewin for being all I could wish for in an agent. Amelia Thorpe for believing in me. Isabel Duffy for making publicity fun. Hannah MacDonald, who is not only an excellent editor, but now, annoyingly, turns out to be a better writer than me.

And of course, this book, like everything else I write, is for Jan.

(Hey, look I know this dedication bangs on a bit, but I'm never going to win an Oscar, and I always fancied doing one of those speeches. So at least I've got that out of my system. Now if you want to hear my list of records for *Desert Island Discs* ...)

By the same author

The Little Book of Stress
The Stocking Filler
The Little Book of Wrong Shui
Stress for Success
The Autobiography of a One Year Old
The Little Book of The Kama Sutra
The Parent's Survival Handbook
Growing Old Disgracefully
University Challenged
Harry Potter and the Philosopher's Stone *

*No, hold on a minute, that was JK Rowling. Damn. I suppose this means I'll have to send the Mercedes back.

**'Deck the halls with boughs of holly,
'tis the season to be jolly …'**

Oh really?

Not enough money, not enough time, not
enough chairs for everyone to sit on. Too many
presents to get, too many relatives to invite, too
many things to get into the oven at the same time.

Face the facts, Christmas is the central festivity
of our over-indulgent lives because beneath the
surface gloss of its glorification of greed it is, in
essence, a celebration of stress.

And stress, as the enlightened among you will
already know, is undoubtedly a Good Thing.

So I urge you to wake up and smell the turkey
curry, embrace the True Meaning Of Christmas,
and do all that you can to encourage the generation
of stress in both yourself and those around you this
Festering Season.

Good luck!

'But It's Only March!'

If you run a large supermarket encourage your customers' festive feelings of joy by putting out Christmas stock earlier and earlier each year.

The Turkey Conundrum

No one really likes turkey. If they did they'd eat it more than once a year. But try not serving it for Christmas lunch and a lot of your guests will be disappointed and feel secretly cheated.

With this kind of muddled thinking at the core of our national psyche is it any wonder that we have little chance of getting rid of the historical anomaly that is the Royal Family?

The Fruitcake Fruitcake

Insist on making your own Christmas cake. Weeks ahead of Christmas Day buy the half a ton of ingredients, plus the assorted cake tins, cooling racks, etc. that you need. Add up the cost and realise it would have been cheaper to go to Harrods and buy their most expensive offering. Press on regardless and spend what seems the best part of a whole day making the damned thing.

Then store said cake till Christmas Day when on first cutting into it you discover that, having left it in the oven for probably 10 seconds too long, you've produced nothing but a very expensive doorstop that's about as moist as the Mojave desert during a particularly dry drought.

All Wrapped Up

Wrap your presents two weeks in advance. Place under tree. Forget to put tags on.

Oh God, Not That Again

At selected moments try to spoil everyone's
Christmas Day by bringing religion into it.

The Festering Season

When visiting friends, slip unwanted turkey,
sprouts or Stilton down the back of radiators.

Sitting Pretty

Encourage merriment and japery around the dining table by surreptitiously decorating everyone's seat with a seasonal and festive holly leaf.

Getting Shirty

Never keep the receipts for any items of clothing that you buy for friends and relatives. That way the ungrateful swines won't be able to change them for something more 'their style', 'their colour' or 'their size' the moment your back is turned.

You're a Right Card, Aren't You?

Card manufacturers, why not cash in on people's goodwill by producing Charity Christmas cards where a ridiculously small amount of the price paid actually gets passed on to the Charity you are so piously supporting?

A Little Light Entertainment

Why not endear yourself to your neighbours by
erecting a spectacular selection of lighting
displays on your house, your roof, your trees and
your front garden, featuring charming Christmas
scenes both religious and secular? Aim for a
combined Blackpool Illuminations and Las Vegas
effect. Only make it far less subtle.

(N.B. This is a particularly effective ploy if your
neighbours are middle class and hence, supposedly, know
all about good taste.)

Ahh, Bless Them

Make sure any children you encounter understand that the true meaning of Christmas is to get as many presents as possible.

'I can't believe it's been a whole year ...'

Send cards to people you contact only once a
year. Suggest that 'we must meet up in the New
Year'.

Know that you never will.

Christmas in the Smallest Room

Replace your loo roll with festive tinsel.

It's Right He Should Suffer

Go round to Aled Jones's house. Screech 'I'm Walking In the Air' through the letter box.

Preferably late at night.

What's It All About?

Throughout the festive season loudly complain that the true meaning has been lost. But never actually do anything religious yourself.

V.C.Arrgh

Assiduously mark all the programmes you want to watch or video in the bumper Christmas TV guide. Count them up and contemplate just how sad you really are.

It's Traditional

Buy a new jar of cranberry sauce
to replace the half-finished one you've
still got in the fridge from last year.

And This Is Me

If you're a celebrity living a life of shameless, almost psychotic attention seeking and excess, throughout the year do everything in your power to distance yourself from the lives of 'ordinary' people. Then at Christmas try to con money out of the public by bringing out an 'autobiography' that 'reveals' that you're just a normal person like everyone else.

Don't Forget the Christmas Puddings

Always buy large boxes of chocolates for friends
that you know are concerned about their weight.

Pucker Up

Amuse your in-laws by sellotaping a sprig of mistletoe to the buckle of your belt when you go round to visit them.

The Fifty Best

Assiduously read all the lists of 'Fifty Best Presents' that the papers and magazines print in the run-up to Christmas. Then contemplate just what a tasteless cheapskate you are when you realise that you don't like any of them except the things you think vastly over-priced.

Oops!

Remember to get, well in advance, the details of last posting dates for overseas cards and gifts from the Post Office. However, forget to post said mail in time.

Some Jokes Are a Little Hard to Stomach

When going round to a friend or relative's house for Christmas lunch, a cheerily wrapped packet of indigestion tablets makes an excellent 'comedy' present that your host will never, ever be 100% sure you meant purely in jest.

Festive Seasoning

Before Christmas lunch unscrew the lid of the salt cellar.

'While shepherds washed their ...'

Store up merriment for your friends and relatives by secretly teaching their young children rude versions of Christmas carols.

Santa's Grotty

While queuing up with your son or daughter to get into Santa's Grotto at a large department store, explain to your offspring that Santa isn't real. Explain in a voice loud enough that nearby (and ideally younger) children can hear, too.

The Good Book

Encourage your children to appreciate the true meaning of Christmas by daily readings from The Good Book. I speak, of course, of the Argos catalogue.

All Present and Correct?

Always remember to get presents for everyone on your list. Except the one person who will feel most snubbed by their omission.

But We Went to Your Parents Last Year!

Never let the fact that *you* chose where you and your partner went for Christmas last year prevent you from trying to have your own way again *this* year.

Bonus Bust-ups

If you're the boss of a company that's doing well, structure Christmas bonus payments so that people doing the same jobs get different payments. Inadvertently leave details of this lying around in the photocopier.

Christmas Cards

If you're the boss of a company that's doing badly, why wait till the New Year to make people redundant?

Seating Plans

If you're arranging the Christmas party at work, always seat people together who don't get on with each other.

Better to Be Safe than Sorry

When decorating a room for the Christmas party at work be sure to discretely display posters explaining the dangers of sexually transmitted diseases amongst the tinsel, balloons and mistletoe.

Hats Off

If you manage a business that has dealings with members of the public, endear yourself to your staff by insisting they wear festive pixie hats topped by flashing red plastic baubles at all time.

Hats Off. (Again.)

The festive red pixie hat for staff members is a particularly productive approach if you happen to run a funeral parlour.

A Time for Laughter

If you're under twenty-five remember to annoy
any relatives older than yourself by pointing out
to them that Morecambe and Wise were actually
really unfunny.

A Present With a Past

Re-wrap and return unwanted and generally crap gifts from last year to the people who gave them to you in the first place.

Plan Ahead

When looking ahead to the hurly-burly inevitably involved in Christmas Day with all the family around, it's very important that you make time for all the things you really need to do and that make Christmas Christmas. Hence, when planning your day be sure to schedule ten minutes every hour for trivial, petty arguments.

How to Deal With the Born-Again Brigade

Ladies, should your hectic preparations be constantly interrupted by smiling born-again Christians and the like knocking on your door, send them on their way by your incontrovertible proof that the whole Christmas story is a fantasy. 'Three wise men? Together in one place? I don't think so.'

How to Deal With the Born-Again Brigade. (Again.)

Should your evangelical door-to-door salesmen be made of sterner stuff, and despite your first efforts to send them packing still insist on spreading the joy of the season, unleash upon them your theological weapon of mass destruction.

Namely concede to them that there is one way that the Three Wise Men story could be true. All you need is a closer examination of the text.

I mean, three men, travelling together, fabulously dressed, one bringing a gift of jewellery and two bringing gifts of, essentially, up-market pot-pourri, trying to get into some backstreet dive called 'The Stable' at way past midnight?

(Oh come on, do you really need a Judy Garland CD playing in the background to get the picture?)

Happy Xmas

There are some people who, on religious grounds, get very upset whenever Christmas is referred to as Xmas. Should you ever encounter such zealots your course of action is clear.

Happy Exmas

Much grief and heartfelt soul-searching can be generated just before Christmas by trying to restart a relationship with a lover that you dumped earlier in the year.

(Extra points are available if the old flame is now happily ensconced in a new relationship.)

Of Course Size Matters

When sent out by your partner to buy a Christmas tree for the home make sure you bring one back that is either way too big or far too small for the room it's going to be in.

It's Not Just Snow that Falls

When positioning a Christmas tree in your living room always try to make sure that it looks secure, but in fact isn't.

Decorating the Tree

Hang all the breakable decorations down at the bottom of the tree where small children can easily reach them.

On the Constantly Contemporary Relevance of the Age-old Christmas Story

Let's face it, God wasn't in love with Mary. And they didn't have anything that could be termed, even in the loosest sense, a relationship. And they certainly weren't married. Indeed, as far as we can make out, God unilaterally chose Mary to carry his son. So the degree to which Mary had a choice in the matter is a tad doubtful, what with an angel announcing the fact to her somewhat out of the blue. I mean it's not as if she even got taken out to dinner first.

Add all these facts together and it becomes clear that the whole Christmas mullarkey is really a somewhat dubious story of totally unregulated IVF, pre-natal sex selection and, it could be argued, surrogate motherhood.

Now what could be more contemporary than that?

All Wrapped Up. (Again.)

Always buy that exceptionally cheap, thin
wrapping paper that they sell down the market.
You know, the type that tears whenever you try
to wrap anything.

Giving Them the Needle

On visits to friends or relatives shake their Christmas trees vigorously when no one is looking.

No One Likes Them

Serve Brussels sprouts.

Veg Out

If your hostess insists on serving you Brussels Sprouts point out to her that they are just premature cabbages. Refuse to eat them on grounds of infanticide.

Christmas Shopping
– to the Victor the Spoils

If ever you needed evidence that all this 'season of goodwill' mullarkey is just a load of old bolleaux you need look no further than the war zone that is your average high street as Christmas approaches.

Three weeks from C-Day things may still be polite round the cash registers, but come the final week all pretence at civilised behaviour disappears quicker than a chocolate éclair at a meeting of Overeaters Anonymous.

For this reason I thought it best, over the next few pages, to share with you some of the techniques you will need to succeed in this Crucible of Cruelty.

The Trip

A rather basic, though effective, technique. It involves the judicious use of a trailing leg or outstretched foot in any crowded shopping environment. Should your victim suspect foul play turn the tables on them by loudly shouting out the phrase 'Ow!' and staring at the clumsy oaf who has so cruelly attempted to maim you.

The Shirt Tug

Essentially a holding technique to buy you some time and help you draw level or overtake an opponent who is going for the same object as you.

The Dive

The Dive is perhaps the most dramatic and effective manoeuvre a seasoned campaigner can execute, as it both implies evil intent on the part of your innocent adversary and directs sympathy and (with any luck) shop assistants to you. Once said shop assistants are worriedly asking if 'you're okay?' it takes but a few winces of (fake) pain to recruit them to your cause and have them do all the heavy lift and shift work for you.

The Elbow

To execute The Elbow correctly, first draw level
with your opponent. Then thrust your elbow
back with all the venom you can muster into
their ribs or abdomen. Now, just as rapidly, shove
your hand into your trouser pocket to remove the
credit card you need to pay for your purchases
and, of course, to provide the perfect alibi for
your elbow action.

The Hand Ball (Or Vinnie J.)

Only to be attempted under the most extreme provocation as it involves the public compression of the privates of your foe.

   Be sure you've reconnoitred at least two escape routes before you even think of attempting such a powerful ploy.

That'll Surprise the Old Bugger

Maximise the chances of Santa getting stuck up the chimney by secretly narrowing the opening.

Splash It All Over

Buy your partner a large, expensive bottle of
perfume or aftershave. Then leave the present in
such a position that it is bound to be knocked
over and broken by a small child.

Practice Makes Perfect

If you are a small child make sure that, in the weeks leading up to Christmas Day, you perfect just the right combination of high-pitched screams and frenzied floorbound body-thrashing-around techniques to create a tantrum of such theatrical potency to unleash when you realise that you haven't got one of the presents on your ludicrously long list that your parents will suddenly realise they have raised an ungrateful, spoiled brat and that maybe there's still time before next Christmas to convert to an ultra-austere form of Islam that makes the Taliban look like an Ibiza-bound plane-load of Club 18–30 party animals.

The Potency of Desire

Another productive technique for small children to employ in stress generation is to see just how far they can push their parents by the persistent and consistent juxtaposition of the word 'I' with the word 'want' in the days, weeks and indeed months leading up to the Great Day of Disappointments.

He's Obviously Never Met Trinny and Susannah

If roped in to be Father Christmas at a small children's party, add a streetwise, contemporary edge to the proceedings by eschewing the traditional garish red attire and opting for a far more slimming black outfit instead.

The Party Season

One sure-fire way to depress friends and workmates is casually, in the course of conversation, to invent fictitious parties that you've been invited to and hence force them to contemplate what dull lives they lead and how unpopular they are.

It's Just People From Work, Dear

If you run a company try and bolster the strength of the marriages and relationships of your employees by insisting that partners aren't invited to the Christmas party and then holding it in a glamorous, romantic hotel that's not at all easy to get back from at two in the morning. Then finesse the technique by telling your staff that you've managed to negotiate a substantial discount for anyone wanting to save the hassle of searching for a cab and book a room.

Cook the Books

This money-saving tip has the benefit of simultaneously annoying bookshops, publishers, and Delia, Nigella, Jamie, and the rest of those thoroughly over-egged 'celebrity' chefs who really are just hyped up home economics teachers. It involves gift selection for those friends and relatives who've suggested they'd really like the latest book, from the latest TV series, of the latest cooking sensation.

If they're honest, what they would really like is one or two, or at most three, recipes said 'star' featured in said TV series. Indeed, if you did buy them the book, those few recipes would be the only pages that ever got used.

Hence, it is but common sense for you to nip down to the bookshop, razor out those particular recipes and give these as the present to your friend or relative.

Treat Yourself To a Christmas Hamper

Save time and money when out food shopping by buying a Christmas hamper of goodies. Then when you get it home and unpack it, discover you don't really fancy half the stuff in it, that it was ludicrously over-priced, and how often are you going to need a wicker basket in the coming year anyway.

A Brief Analysis of The Semantics of the Word 'Hamper'

Ponder the fact that an alternative meaning of the word 'hamper' is 'hinder'.

How to Drive People Dipsy (Or La-La)

If you're the producer of a brainwashingly successful children's TV series, record and release an inane but infectiously catchy single with a spurious Christmas theme that subsequently dominates the airwaves and camps out at the number one spot for upwards of a month.

Not All Streets Are of the Same Quality

Buy boxes of Quality Street as presents for your nearest and dearest. But before wrapping them up and handing them over, secretly take out and eat all the purple ones.

It's Like the First Cuckoo of Spring for the Consumer Age ...

Organise a sweepstake with your friends on the first sighting of a Christmas commercial on TV. Put a fiver on it each, and an occurrence that is fundamentally deeply depressing suddenly takes on a completely new and potentially lucrative dimension.

Sometimes Christmas Doesn't Only Begin at Home

Endeavour to add some 'true meaning' to your Christmas by resolving to help out at a homeless hostel on Christmas Day. Then fail to do anything about it until it is way too late and have to confront the fact that while in your own head you like to think of yourself as a 'caring' person, in reality you're as shallow as a puddle and as selfish as a politician.

Setting Light to the Pudding

Diet books make excellent gifts for overweight friends and relatives.

It's Nice to Have a Reminder of This Christmas in the Months and Years to Come

Ladies, really build up your expectations of festive fun by buying yourself a fab, and far too expensive, little frock to wear to all the parties that you're going to be invited to. Then the very first time you wear it spill something on it that you're never able to really successfully clean off.

My, how you'll laugh!

Charades

This is an ever-popular festive season game that is well worthwhile practising in private ahead of the actual day. The aim of the game is to communicate, through your actions and general demeanour, the fact that you are overjoyed by the appearance of your partner's boring, voracious, hard-to-please and eager-not-to-help relatives, who turn up either way too early or far too late on Christmas Day.

End This Panettone Madness Now!

Why not prove the cutting edge-ness of your European cultural credentials by turning up at friends' homes that you've been invited to with a gift of an excessively boxed and wrapped panettone. Your host will then be forced to smile in fake gratitude and add it to the rapidly increasing Alpine range of this type of cakery that is gathering in the kitchen. And it's not as if anyone will get round to eating them before they go stale. After all, they're nothing more than oversized buns that the canny Italian baking industry has conned other parts of Europe into paying well over the odds for.

(What better metaphor could there be for Christmas as a whole?)

It All Collapsed Like a House of Cards

When hanging Christmas cards as a decoration around your home always remember not to fix the ribbon or string they're hanging on very securely. That way they will constantly fall to the floor, enabling you to indulge in a satisfying bout of traditional Christmas Swearing.

'It's gonna be lonely this Christmas …'

Ladies, this Christmas, if you are happily married or ensconced in a relationship, make a habit of hanging out with work colleagues who aren't and regaling them with the coupley delights that you and your beau have to look forward to over the festive season.

A Moment of Realisation

Face up to the depressing fact that you are gullible by watching TV shows described as 'Christmas Specials' expecting them to be 'special'.

Stuck in a Sticky Place

If you are a manufacturer of sticky tape, why not add to the general fun and frolics of Christmas by making sure that the end of the sticky tapes you produce always completely disappears from sight whenever a piece has been cut from the roll?

'Write a letter to Santa? Yeah,
OK Grandad, I'll just dip my quill
in crushed beetle juice and get right
on it!'

Kids, why not both annoy your parents and save
time by resisting their attempts to get you to
'write a letter to Santa' and informing them that
you've already texted the old geezer the following
msg:

snd mr stff

From Bling! Bling! to Bing Bing

If you've got grandchildren why not endear yourselves to them this Christmas by not getting the foul-mouthed Gangsta Rap CD they requested, but buying them a nice seasonal Bing Crosby album instead?

The Top of the Tree Dilemma – a Fairy Or a Star?

Why not resolve the long-running dispute with a thoroughly modern compromise? Just stick the cover from the latest Elton John CD at the top of the tree and keep both 'camps' happy.

Well, Isn't It About Time the Miserable Old Git Wrote Back?

Every year millions of children write letters to Santa. But he never replies. I mean, how disheartening must that be for the kiddies? Why not reassure them that their missives have at least reached Santa, by typing out the following acknowledgement slip and posting it through the letter boxes of homes in your neighbourhood where you know children live:

Mr Claus thanks you for your recent communication and notes with interest the requests you have made. However, due to his ever-increasing workload at this time of year and the poor performance of his heavily IT-biased investment portfolio, he feels that it is highly unlikely that he will be able to provide any of the items you specify. Mr Claus apologises for any disappointment that this may cause.

After All, ''Tis the season to be jolly'

Another sure-fire way to wind people up is to be unceasingly jolly about everything to do with Christmas. Just endlessly bang on about how much you love the hustle and bustle, the shopping, the cooking, the card sending, the house decorating, the tree dressing, the expeditions to buy presents, the wrapping of the presents, and the outrageous expectations and demands of the already over-indulged children.

People will really hate you for it.

Still a Ton Left

Buy one of those really big wheels of Stilton secure in the knowledge that in any gathering of twenty people only three actually like the stuff so it'll live in your fridge for weeks on end where even lifting the smallest corner of the miles of clingfilm you wrap it in will release a fragrance so pungent that seconds later UN weapons inspectors will burst through your front door in search of biological weapons of mass destruction.

Salmon Chanted Evening

Buy a whole side of smoked salmon. Watch in horror as at least a third of it shrivels up and dries out, when after a couple of days you're sick of the stuff.

'Oh look, how Christmassy – someone's scattered glittery snow underneath the car door!'

A great way for your presents to be a real surprise for the people who eventually get them is to leave them all wrapped up on the back seat of your car while you do that traditional bit of last-minute shopping.

Why Do You Think They Call It Advent?

Before you get in a state over how much of the media is saturated by adverts for an avalanche of Christmas excess in every shape, form and size, consider the sobering fact that another name for the festive season is 'advent'. Which, when you break it down semantically, must mean the seasonal celebration when all manner of 'ads' get to be 'vented' on the public. How appropriate.

It's Not Only Children Who Suspend Their Disbelief at Christmas

'Yes Madam, I know that forty pounds seems a lot for a small jar of white gunk that's been cooked up in a *laboratoire** but it really does make a "visible" difference and if you can't pamper yourself at Christmas, then when can you? Oh yes, it is a lovely box …'

* Interesting how a foreign language can transform a word that in English would otherwise reek of spotty schoolboys, Bunsen burners, mad scientists and cut-up rats into something redolent of a world of cleanliness, purity and beauty.

Something to Think About

Recently, as people increasingly already have all the stuff they could ever want, the massed forces of the industries that try to sell us presents at Christmas have, in panic, expanded what they have to offer us to include 'Experiences'. Hence you can now give your loved one, for example, a spa day or a racing car day, a gourmet cooking course or a flight in a hot-air balloon. All are 'Experiences' that aim to enrich the life of the recipient. And, more importantly, aim to enrich the bank balance of the company flogging said 'Experience'.

In response to this totally unnecessary colonisation of these virgin territories by the voracious empire-building forces of Christmas may I suggest a different 'Experience' for you to give on Christmas Day. It is the 'Conceptual Art Experience'.

For this you need to get yourself a large empty box and beautifully wrap it in the finest Christmas wrapping paper you can find. Then give it to your loved one for Christmas.

At one stroke you will have created an 'Experience' that is thought-provoking, profound, anti-consumerist, satirical, and deeply pretentious. What other present could offer so much?

On top of all that it's dead cheap. And when your bemused loved one laughs indulgently at 'your little joke' and then asks, in vain, where their real present is, it will prove relationship-shatteringly annoying.

It's in the Bag

When out buying Christmas presents always carry at least one more bag crammed full of gifts than you can realistically handle. Then attempt to board a crowded bus or tube train.

It's in Case it Looks Like Rain, Dear

Eschew the traditional gift for your loved one this year. Buy a sensible and practical collapsible umbrella instead.

Honestly, It'll Be Empty

Always do your present shopping on the last weekend before Christmas. Preferably in Croydon.

It's About Time You Told the Truth

If you are the Queen, before you record your Christmas Message get well mullahed on Lambrini and Bailey's then sit yourself down with a large doner (including chilli sauce) and finally tell the public what you've really been thinking all these years.

Why Should Rudolph Be the Only One With a Red Nose?

An excess of alcohol is a sure-fire way of increasing the strains and stresses of a family Christmas.

Don't Forget the Fun of the Last-Minute Present

There's always one. One person for whom you forgot to get a present. You forgot because the person in question is usually not one of the most important in your life. However, at the last minute, you realise you do need to get them something. So you hare round the shops. And because it is the last minute, you haven't got enough time (or energy) to find something appropriate. So you end up spending far too much money. All of which makes it a present that provides untold opportunities to wind yourself up about and that nails the lie that 'it is better to give than to receive'. That's because when you do hand it over you won't ever be able to totally suppress that nagging feeling of resentment.

And that's why it's one of the true classics of the whole Christmas stress generation milieu. One to be savoured.

Midnight Massacre

Make your annual trip to church for Midnight Mass. Try to jolly everyone along by singing 'Agadoo' in the quiet bits and starting a conga.

The Future Is Orange

Confuse and perplex your guests by serving tangerines, satsumas and clementines together in the same bowl.

Why Not Surprise Your Wife and Take a Tip from Prince Albert This Christmas?

Prince Albert, it is commonly acknowledged, was responsible for importing the tradition of decorating a fir tree as a central part of the seasonal festivities. The enlightened amongst you will also know that his other claim to fame was, allegedly, to have a piercing, and a ring positioned in the, let's just say, chipolata that dangled between his Brussels sprouts.

Well gents, seeing as the Christmas tree proved such an enduring hit, why not try the Prince's other innovation and see if that doesn't bring a smile to the face of your lady wife of a yuletide evening. And why not really get into the festive spirit by attaching a snippet of tinsel to said ring and see if that doesn't tickle her fancy?

A Suitable Riposte

Ladies, surprise your partner on Christmas Eve by soberly telling them that you've discovered a great way to put the sparkle back into your bedroom canoodlings. Then go off to spend the night with your lover.

'Is it Christmas yet?'

Parents, why not subvert the age-old, and deeply annoying, tradition of your kids waking up early on Christmas Day and pestering you for their presents while you're still half asleep, by setting your alarm clock for three in the morning, then rushing into *their* rooms, waking *them* up and pestering them while they're still half asleep. Let's see how much they like it.

106

'You're not wearing that!'

Kids, why not endear yourself to your parents by wearing your grungiest or tartiest clothes on Christmas Day? How could they fail to love your spirited show of youthful independence?

'Ahh look, he's on a drip ...'

If you're the commissioning editor of a TV channel make sure to send a camera crew and a has-been TV presenter down to the children's ward of a hospital for a live broadcast on Christmas morning. But try not to feature anyone with anything incurable.

Farther Christmas

Remember that the farther you have to travel on Christmas Day the more likely you are to argue.

Plan your day accordingly.

Can We Open the Presents Yet?

Families always traditionally open their presents at the same particular time each Christmas Day. Encourage a little light-hearted debate by first suggesting, then insisting on, a completely different time 'just for a change'.

Grate Expectations

Wrap a small, cheap present in a large
bicycle-shaped package.
Give to a small child.

Tied Up

If you are a toy manufacturer ensure that the toys you produce are held in place in their boxes by so many plastic-coated metal ties that the child receiving the toy will be subjected to an increasingly bad-tempered barrage of 'wait a minutes' from an increasingly frustrated parent trying to release the damn thing.

When Christmas Snaps

Why not fail to capture the joy on your children's faces as they open their presents by forgetting to get a film for your camera?

Sensible, Sensible, Sensible

When visiting friends or relatives with young children you can't go wrong with an educational book as a present.

Cardigan Arrest

If your mother/granny/maiden aunt gives you a truly horrendous Christmas jumper/cardigan/balaclava, fake a dramatic heart attack and in the ensuing mêlée rip the offending garment asunder.

Computer Games

When a young relative has specified the particular game he wants for his games console encourage him to appreciate the value of money, and hence make him the envy of his mates, by getting him a cheaper alternative.

A Novel Approach

Remember the batteries.
Forget the present.

Suddenly the Christmas Festivities Went Rapidly Downhill

If you're visiting a home this Christmas where young children live why not buy them a gift of that traditional festive favourite – a sled. Such a present will be an undoubted great hit and will guarantee that:

a. you will enjoy a snow-free Christmas;

b. you will get the chance to sample the tea- and coffee-making facilities available at the casualty department of the local hospital.

It's the Thought that Counts

Practise saying 'oh, that's nice' to perfect the barely perceptible glimpse of insincerity so valuable when unwrapping presents.

'You shouldn't have'

Instigate a 'token present only' rule between yourself and your partner. Then make them feel inadequate and mean by buying them something really expensive.

You Really Shouldn't Have

What wife/female partner would not be charmed at Christmas by something useful for the house?

Trivial Pursuit

Try and get everyone into a spirit of fun by insisting they all sit down and play a board game that no one is interested in and whose rules take almost forty-five minutes to read and understand.

A Throw-away Technique

When tidying away discarded wrapping paper into a black bin liner after the present-opening frenzy always remember to slip into the rubbish one of the smaller, more valuable gifts.

Charity Begins at Home

Invite elderly neighbours who live on their own over for Christmas lunch. Forget to tell them that you've changed your plans and are going to your mum's instead.

Spare a Thought for Those Less Fortunate Than Yourself

Just the one thought. No point in making those bastards complacent.

'You children are so ungrateful, we didn't get half so many things for Christmas when we were young!'

Remember how annoying it was when your parents said this to you when you were little? Well, it's going to be just as annoying for your kids when you start saying it to them.

Enjoy!

'Maybe he'll ring ...'

This is another admirable stress-inducing ploy
that is primarily available to young (and, sadly,
not so young) single women. However, it does
take a little planning and forethought to arrange.
Basically, in order to maximise your potential for
stress and depression during Christmas, start an
affair with an older married work colleague at
some time in the year leading up to it.

Then as the season of goodwill approaches,
you will find ample opportunity to wallow in
self-pity and plummeting self-esteem as your
lover puts his family first and asks you to
'understand'.

What bliss!

The Real Magic of Christmas

You'll be amazed how quickly your money (and your patience) disappears.

Frosty's Not Just a Snowman

Turkey defrosting instructions are only guidelines. Improvise your own approach for a more spontaneous take on Christmas lunch timings.

'Woo-ooo-oooh! Woo-ooo-ooooh!'

Parents, why not try to recapture a taste of a simpler, bygone Christmas age by dragging your ungrateful teenage brats away from their Playstations and bedroom DVD players and getting them to sit in a darkened living room with the whole family while you tell scary Victorian ghost stories? Boy, will they love that. Especially if they've got friends round at the time.

Just Common Sense Really

Save time and washing up by stuffing the turkey with Christmas pudding.

One Great Way to Really Enjoy a Panto

Go to the panto at your local theatre. Liven up
the proceedings by encouraging all the children
present to shout 'Has been!' whenever selected
members of the cast appear on the stage.

Panto. (Part Two.)

Should cast members object to being heckled
with shouts of 'Has been!', up the stakes by
training the children in the audience to shout
'Behind you!' whenever you shout out the query
'Where's your career?'

Deck the Halls

Save money on a festive wreath for your front door by nipping over the wall of the local cemetery after closing time.

I'm Dreaming of a White Christmas

Try to bring a contemporary, urban, streetwise edge to your festive season by first styling your hair into that oh-so-cool Hoxton Fin, then spending all the money you set aside for presents on your very trendy cocaine habit.

Getting the Bird

Wait until your hostess has served you a large plate of turkey, then remember that you are a vegetarian.

Snow Joke

Avoid using expensive fake snow to decorate your windows. Instead use up that white gloss paint you've got left over from doing the skirting boards.

Silent Night. Yo!

Bring a traditional Christmas-time activity bang
up to date by going round the neighbours with a
ghetto blaster and a CD of carol singing.
Serenade them at full volume.

Your Goose Is Cooked

For a change avoid turkey this Christmas and cook a goose instead. No one likes goose and as it is invariably rich and greasy it will combine incredibly uncomfortably with the surfeit of other food that comprises the traditional Christmas Day gorge-athon.

The Shopping Trip Tip

When your partner returns knackered and
carrier-bag-laden from the 'Christmas Present
Shopping Trip From Hell' help lighten their
mood by telling them where they could have got
the presents cheaper.

On the Constantly Contemporary Relevance of the Age-old Christmas Story. Part Two

So you thought the stress-inducing complications of how to sensitively handle step-children and, indeed, step-parenthood was purely a phenomenon of the post-permissive society we now find ourselves living in? Well, think again.

I mean look at it from Joseph's point of view. There you are all excited because you're expecting your first-born. What's more, just to make the happy event all the more perfect, it looks like the little fellow might just turn up in time for Christmas. Then the wife breaks the awful news that it's not your sprog.

So, being a man used to working with your hands you resolve to give the blighter who got the Mrs up the duff a good kicking, at which point she chips in with the news that the geezer in question is 'not from round here'. Indeed he's not from round anywhere on account of him being God.

Now how inadequate and emasculated does that make you feel?

But you love your wife. So, after much heartache and soul-searching, you resolve to raise and love the kid as your own. And you've just managed to swallow your pride and get to the night of the actual birth without any residual bitterness tainting what is going to be a truly joyous, private, family occasion when it all goes decidedly avocado-shaped.

First a load of uninvited shepherds turn up saying an angel sent them. Then you look out the window and spot a bloody great star hovering like a police helicopter over the stable you're staying in. And then, guided by this celestial equivalent of the McDonald's golden arches, not one, not two, but three kings turn up, sent by God, bearing totally over-the-top gifts.

In fact, so over-the-top are the gifts that in no time at all it is completely forgotten that you spent hours of your precious spare time carving a tiny set of wooden animals for your new-born son. But then isn't that the typical lot of the step-parent? You do all the work, make all the arrangements, have all the responsibility, then the absent parent sends over some ridiculously over-expensive present, hence staking a claim to be a truly generous, caring parent, when in actual fact all they are doing is assuaging their own guilt and hoping to buy their child's love with money.

And you thought the Christmas story lacked contemporary relevance.

The EastEnders Approach

If you have any momentous news to break to your family e.g. that you're having an affair, are gay, or that you've recently discovered that the woman you thought was your mother isn't your mother and that your real mother was, in fact, your father before he/she had that sex-change operation that he/she financed by selling heroin to schoolchildren, do it during lunch on Christmas Day. Preferably just as the hot gravy is coming round.

The Hat Trick

Should arguments or unhappiness mar your table during Christmas lunch, completely change the mood of the gathering by insisting that everyone wears, and isn't allowed to remove, the hilarious paper hats that come with the Christmas crackers. How could that fail to cheer everyone up?

'It's gonna be lonely this Christmas ...' (a Slight Refrain)

If you're an uncle or aunt of an unattached niece enliven the conversation over Christmas lunch by asking them if they've got a boyfriend yet.
(This is an especially potent technique for nieces in their thirties).

'Did you know that every snowflake is completely different?'

When conversation lulls around the table during Christmas lunch bore every one rigid with useless, uninteresting, unprovable facts.

Hippy Christmas Everybody

Another sure-fire way to annoy the more traditionally minded of your friends and family is to invite everyone to share your joss-stick-infused, nut-roast-laden, winter solstice celebration. Cheesecloth dresses, tie-dyed T-shirts and barefoot cavorting to your Best of Steeleye Span CD all being compulsory, of course.

They'll Never Know There Wasn't One in There

Wait until all the Christmas pudding has been eaten, then ask, 'Who found the sixpence?'

Questions, Questions

Aunts and uncles, endear yourselves to your
young nieces and nephews by asking them how
they're getting on at school and remarking upon
how much they've grown.

Questions, Questions, Questions

Aunts and uncles, keep up old traditions and
endear yourselves to your university-student
nieces and nephews by asking them how they're
getting on at school and remarking upon how
much they've grown.

There's No Better Way to Hasten a Republic

Insist that everyone sits down and listens to the Queen's Christmas Message. (And insist everyone stands up for the national anthem.)

The Season of Good Will

At family gatherings remind elderly relatives that it's very sensible to make a will. If they appear somewhat reluctant chivvy them along by handing out the will forms you've brought along to 'help them out'.

A Partridge? In a Pear Tree??

Inappropriate, impractical gifts are always winners in the stress-generation stakes. Heighten the degree of discomfort felt by the recipient by making the gifts excessively expensive.

'Call That Music?'

Watch the Christmas edition of *Top Of the Pops*. Lament the lack of real songs/tunes/stars. Then contemplate the fact that you've turned into your dad/mum.

Film Fun

TV schedulers, remember to screen the only
decent film you've secured for the festive period
at a time on Christmas Day when hardly anyone
will get the chance to watch it all the way
through.

It's a Wonderful Life

Really?

Force family and friends to watch some boring old black and white movie on the telly on account of it being a 'classic'.

Why It's Best to Be Wary of the Grape and the Grain at Office Christmas Parties

It's all because imbibing heartily of the products of the grape and the grain can all too easily lead you to the dubious 'delights' of the grope and the groan. The 'grope' is fairly self-explanatory; the 'groan' is the experience that engulfs you as your hangover clears the next morning and you wake to the nausea-inducing panic of 'Oh my God! I did what? With whom? And who saw it all?'

Why the Christmas 'I've Got Nothing To Wear' Crisis Is Never Really Understood by Boyfriends and Husbands

It's because they've never got their heads round the fact that the people you're dressing to impress isn't really them, but your girlfriends.

Sherry? Sherry? No one Likes Sherry

Annoy guests by offering them a traditional glass of sherry. No one likes sherry. In fact the only person who drinks the stuff regularly is Father Christmas. And as that's all he's offered (along with a couple of mince pies) after he's dragged over a sackful of presents for you all the way from Lapland, it probably explains why he only turns up once a year.

It's Just As Well There Are No Other Sleighs Up There

Come to think of it, if Santa has a glass of sherry at every house he visits he's pretty soon going to be as well-oiled as an oil well. I mean, what kind of example is that for kids today?

The Last Post

There's nothing more annoying than getting a card in the last few days before Christmas from someone you didn't send one to. Frankly, they do it just to make you feel bad. Selfish bastards.

Drive Them Nuts

Put empty shells back in the bowl with the nuts.

Why the Big Christmas Day Movie Is Always a Disappointment

Like so many of the traditions associated with Christmas, the Big Movie is one that is hopelessly out of date and irritatingly irrelevant. That's because its real potency goes back to the days when the only way to see a film was either at the cinema when it was released or what seemed several years later when it was eventually shown on TV. In such circumstances the first screening on TV of a great film you'd only seen once, or had even missed when it was in the cinemas, was indeed something to look forward to and savour.

However, those times have long since passed. These days a film gets released in the cinema, next goes onto satellite T.V., then arrives at the video rental shop, then is for sale on video, followed by DVD with extra bits – and only then, after every last potential viewer has been given every last chance to see it and pay repeatedly for the privilege, is it flogged to terrestrial TV.

So by the time a Big Movie makes it to the much-fanfared Christmas Day TV screening it usually has about as much allure as the nineteenth repeat screening of that rather ludicrous episode of *Murder She Wrote* where it turns out, my how we laughed, the butler actually did it.

But still the TV companies trumpet their Christmas Day booty centrepiece like they've suddenly discovered, and are about to share with us, the totally unexpected and life-changing experience of the fourth part of *The Lord of the Rings* trilogy.

Yeah, right guys. Who do you think you're kidding?

Why Should the Traditional Boxing Day Hunt Only Be Available to Country Folk?

It has long been customary for certain people in certain parts of this fair and sceptic isle to blow away the cobwebs of over-indulgence that the festive season encourages, by donning red coats, black hats and shiny boots, and setting off on horseback, on Boxing Day, to try to hound, harry and rip to shreds one of Basil Brush's country cousins. (Obviously the whole 'goodwill to all men' hoo-hah not really being applicable to foxes.)

But why should these country folk have all the fun? Surely the rest of the Boxing Day nation, uncomfortably bloated like a foie gras goose, could do with a little exercise that a hunt of some sort would encourage. But what to hunt, that's the question. Below I make a few suggestions that could easily become a traditional activity for almost any household, in almost any part of the country, in the torpor, disappointment and general turkey sandwichedness of Boxing Day.

Possible Things to Search For On an Alternative Boxing Day Hunt:
1. Batteries
2. The receipt for the present you didn't want
3. The missing piece of the high-tech present you bought your kids without which the damned thing doesn't actually work
4. The TV remote control
5. The nutcracker
6. The purple Quality Street
7. A programme on the TV you actually want to watch
8. The Alka Seltzer
9. The magic of the Christmases you had as a child
10. Meaning

How to Avoid the Post-Christmas Blues

You know that dreadful sinking feeling that engulfs you after Christmas when it suddenly dawns on you that there's nothing more to get stressed or depressed about? Well, one sure-fire way to avoid it is to hotfoot it round the sales as soon as they start and find out how much cheaper all the presents are that you shelled out a fortune on just a few days ago.

A Date to Remember

Historically speaking we celebrate the birth of Jesus on the wrong day. The early Christians in Egypt regarded the 6 January as the date of the Nativity. The Western church, being somewhat pragmatic in nature, moved the date to the 25 December as this was when the heathen masses they were so keen to convert celebrated their great festivals marking the Birth of the Sun. So 25 December is actually a pagan festival.

All of which is deeply annoying ammunition to use should you encounter anyone who bangs on about the true religious significance of Christmas being lost in a landslide of commercialisation. After all, what could be more commercial than changing the birthday of the Son of God just so you can attract more punters to your fledgling religion?

Mulled Wine Mullarkey

Should you find, by some strange oversight, a full-on wine snob turning up at your home during the festive season, smugly proffering a vastly expensive bottle of Chateau Pompousarse, bring a smile to his visage by sticking its contents in a bowl with a sachet of mulling spice and bunging it in the microwave for a couple of minutes.

If You're Sick of Turkey, Try a Joint

When you're at your wit's end over what to do with the seemingly never-ending supply of turkey left-overs try this recipe for Turkey Hash.

1. Shred turkey remnants into small pieces.
2. Mix with marijuana.
3. Roll up in a Rizla and smoke at your leisure.

Dream On

Unrealistic expectations are always a winner at Christmas. Try to encourage as many of them as you possibly can.

Especially For Sam and Ella

Prevent the perennial dry turkey problem
by serving it raw.

What a Carve Up

When having Christmas lunch round at your in-laws' help out by insisting on carving the turkey just to give your father-in-law a break from the family tradition of doing it every year.

What a Cava Up

Alternatively, when having Christmas lunch round at your in-laws' impress them with your common-sense approach to money by bringing round a bottle of Cava instead of champagne.

'Oh … yes … he … is …'

It's an easy mistake to make, but one guaranteed to generate stress all round. Instead of taking your kids to see a panto take them to see some Pinter. Try to make the best of your error by encouraging them to get everyone to join in with some traditional audience participation.

The Snowman

Parents, another great way of causing upset and mayhem this festive season is suggesting to your kids, at the merest dusting of snow, that you all go out and build a snowman. The key here is to forget that we rarely get enough snow, or snow that hangs around long enough, to build a snowman of any decent size. In truth you'll be lucky if there's enough of the stuff to build a snow-dwarf.

Your best bet is to act like a newly elected government that, in the cold light of the fiscal realities it 'discovers', has to scale down its manifesto commitments. Hence build a snow-gerbil. And then have fun trying to convince your kids that it's just as good as the full-on, full-size snowman that they were expecting.

Who Wants to Auld Hands Anyway?

Be more positive. Definitely forget old acquaintances and never bring them to mind.

'On the thirteenth day of Christmas ...'

This is the refrain that is always omitted from the old Christmas song. And for good reason. Because it reveals too much of the truth about what lies behind the generosity and largesse of the festive period. I reprint the lines here for your consideration.

> 'On the thirteenth day of Christmas I sent to my true love, a note saying, "So you think I'm so shallow that you can buy my love with material goods? Get lost, creep. I'm not the bimbo you think I am. (But I'm keeping the rings.)"'

Of course, the other reason these lines may not often be sung is that, poetically speaking, they don't scan particularly well. But the sentiment is clear and, I would argue, increasingly relevant today.

A Little More Light Entertainment

Plan ahead for stress creation next Christmas.
When you take the fairy lights down from the
tree, refrain from carefully coiling them up.
Instead just sling them higgledy-piggledy in the
box. That way when you get them out next year
you'll have hours of pleasure ahead of you
untangling the little buggers.

Not Everyone Has Christmas Day Off

Never forget that Christmas is a time when
charitable thoughts should feature in your life.
For example, not everyone has the luxury of a
holiday on Christmas Day. Some people have to
work. So spare a thought for these unfortunate
people. The thought you should spare is this:

'Suckers!'

Boxing Clever Day

When confronted with a big box of chocolates, steal the good ones from the second layer before the first layer has been finished.

Another Heart-warming Christmas Myth Nailed for the Irritating Canard It Really Is

Apparently, one Christmas on the front line during the First World War, the bloodied and mud-spattered squaddies of the British and German armies emerged from their respective trenches and engaged in a comradely game of football.

All together now … 'Ahhhhh!' What a lovely, lovely image.

And that is why, despite the carnage all around them, both sides came to their senses. Realised that the war was meaningless. Decided to call it a draw. Ended the Europe-wide gore-fest early. Refused to fight each other in the Second World War. And played all subsequent football games between these two mighty nations in a fraternal atmosphere of warmth, love and respect. And that's the real power of Christmas.

Why Red and White Are the Traditional Colours of Christmas

It's nothing to do with Santa's outfit. Or robins perched on snowy branches. It's something far more basic and much more profound. Red is the colour your finances end up in after the festive season. And white is the colour you go when you figure out how long it's going to take you to pay off your debts.

Isn't It About Time We Started Dreaming of a Green Christmas?

What better way to symbolise the true effects that the grossly over-consumptive festival of Christmas has on our natural world than by killing a tree, 'decorating' it with gaudy baubles and lights, then sticking it in our 'living' rooms and watching it rot?

It's Such a Magical Time For Children

After all, who can deny the magic of being overwhelmed with so many toys that they don't really appreciate any of them and consequently the only message they receive is that we live in a society that worships greed and excess and that's why we make the celebration of these values the centrepiece of our biggest festivity of the year?

Bah, Humbug

If that last bit of advice strikes a chord, reflect on the depressing fact that if he turned up now both yourself and many others would greet Scrooge as a pin-up, not a party pooper.

The Real Problem Isn't that It's Only Once a Year, But that It's Every Bloody Year

Loath though I am to do it, I thought that as a final-ish entry in this subversive little tome I might make a relatively simple suggestion that would perhaps go some way to improving the overblown stressfest that is Christmas.

Why not celebrate it every other year?

Wouldn't that make it a bit more special? Wouldn't that make it into something you really looked forward to? And, perhaps most importantly of all, wouldn't that make it a whole heap cheaper?

And Such a Magical Time for Adults

There is, of course, one way to have a truly magical Christmas. Just disappear out of the country the week before the twenty-fifth, and don't reappear until the week after the first.

And Finally

God, if you're out there, why not really scare the sprouts out of everyone by turning up unannounced on Christmas Day and explaining what you really had in mind?

About the Author (And Why You Should Buy More of His Books)

Hey, he's a really nice guy. Really nice. And on top of all that he's getting away with this writing mullarkey. He doesn't work very hard, but he makes a living. And he makes a living making people laugh. Now how fab is that? The problem is he's paranoid that at any minute someone official looking is going to turn up and shout 'Oi, you! Get a proper job.' And the thing is he wants to avoid that day as long as possible. And that's where you can help. If you buy lots of his books, and give them as gifts to your friends, relatives and absolute strangers you pass in the street there's an outside chance he'll never ever have to get a proper job again. Which, on the whole, is a good thing for all concerned as you really wouldn't want him driving any bus you were travelling on, or coming round to fix your toilet.

Growing Old Disgracefully is great to give to your parents. *The Parent's Survival Handbook* or *The Autobiography Of a One Year Old* are great for anyone who's got small kids. The little books on *Stress, Wrong Shui* and *The Kama Sutra* only cost a few quid and so you could even afford to give them to people you don't really like. And *University Challenged* is great for students. The best book, however, is *The Stocking Filler*. But unfortunately that's out of print.

All Ebury titles are available in good bookshops or via mail order

TO ORDER (please tick)

The Little Book of Stress	£2.50	❏
The Little Book of Wrong Shui	£2.50	❏
Stress for Success	£2.50	❏
The Little Book of The Kama Sutra	£2.50	❏
Autobiography of a One Year Old	£5.99	❏
The Parent's Survival Handbook	£3.99	❏
Growing Old Disgracefully	£4.99	❏
University Challenged	£4.99	❏

PAYMENT MAY BE MADE USING ACCESS, VISA, MASTERCARD, DINERS CLUB, SWITCH AND AMEX OR CHEQUE, EUROCHEQUE AND POSTAL ORDER (STERLING ONLY)

CARD NUMBER: ....

EXPIRY DATE: .... SWITCH ISSUE NO: ....

SIGNATURE: ....

PLASE ALLOW £2.50 FOR POST AND PACKAGING FOR THE FIRST BOOK AND £1.00 THEREAFTER

ORDER TOTAL: £   (INC P&P)

ALL ORDERS TO:

EBURY PRESS, BOOKS BY POST, TBS LIMITED, COLCHESTER ROAD, FRATING GREEN, COLCHESTER, ESSEX CO7 7DW, UK

TELEHONE: 01206 256 000
FAX: 01206 255 914

NAME:

ADDRESS:

Please allow 28 days for delivery.
❏ Please tick box if you do not wish to receive any additional information
Prices and availability subject to change without notice.